The Grammar Plan

BOOK 1

60 Grammar Worksheets for English and ESL Students

PARTS OF SPEECH

Nouns
Count/Noncount Nouns
Verbs
Adjectives
Comparative and Superlative Adjectives
Adverbs

Brian Giles

www.stickyball.net

Table of Contents

Part 1 – Nouns — page 1

Part 2 – Count / Noncount Nouns — page 10

Part 3 – Verbs — page 21

Part 4 – Subjects and Verbs — page 30

Part 5 – Adjectives — page 38

Part 6 – Comparative and Superlative Adjectives — page 47

Part 7 – Adverbs — page 59

Part 8 – Appendix and Answer Key — page 67

Introduction

The Grammar Plan – Book 1: Parts of Speech is intended as an introductory book for younger, beginner-level English and ESL students. The worksheets in this book introduce the following parts of speech: **Nouns, Count/Noncount Nouns, Verbs, Adjectives, Comparative/Superlative Adjectives, and Adverbs.**

This book is primarily a book of worksheets. Each worksheet, however, contains explanations and examples of the different grammar points written in **clear, simple** English, so that young learners should be able to understand the content and the instructions without relying on explanations from the teacher.

The worksheets in **The Grammar Plan** progress slowly and steadily. When new or difficult information is presented, the worksheets are relatively simple, including identification and recognition exercises. Then, the worksheets become gradually more complex, requiring learners to understand and apply the grammar points being taught.

As a long-time ESL teacher, I have developed and used these worksheets in large classes as well as with private, one-on-one students. The worksheets in this book are very effective at getting students to understand English grammar without being overwhelmed.

If you find this book useful, try out **Book 2: Tenses**, which introduces the basic English tenses, including Present, Past, Future, and Present Continuous Tense, in clear and simple English worksheets.

Good luck, and good grammar!

The material in this book is Copyright 2009 by Brian Giles. All Rights Reserved. Unauthorized copying or distribution is prohibited without the expressed written consent of the author.

The Grammar Plan

Part 1

Nouns

Nouns (1)

Nouns are **people**, **places**, or **things**. <u>You can see and touch most nouns.</u>

people	places	things
the teacher	the classroom	a pencil
my mother	the park	a car
John	England	a cat
the doctor	a department store	a house

Circle the nouns in the sentences below:

1. I want to go to the department store.

2. The doctor and the teacher are in the car.

3. There is a big book in the classroom.

4. My cat likes to sit on the bed.

5. My house is in England.

6. I want to buy some medicine.

7. You can see animals in a zoo.

8. Hi Elle. Your dress is very cute.

Nouns (2)

Nouns are **people**, **places**, or **things**. <u>You can see and touch most nouns.</u>

people	places	things
the teacher	the classroom	a pencil
my mother	the park	a car
John	England	a cat
the doctor	a department store	a house

Write a noun in the blank to complete each sentence:

1. I want to go to _____.

2. The _____ and the _____ are in the car.

3. There is a big _____ in the classroom.

4. _____ likes to sit on the bed.

5. My _____ is in England.

6. I want to buy some _____.

7. You can see _____ in a zoo.

8. Hi Elle. Your _____ is very cute.

Nouns (3)

Nouns can be **singular** or **plural**:

Singular means there is **only one**:
(You usually add "a" or "an" before a singular noun.)
- a car
- a school
- a hat
- an apple
- an elephant
- an umbrella

Plural means there are **two or more**:
(You add "s" or "es" at the end of most plural nouns.)
- cars
- schools
- hats
- apples
- elephants
- umbrellas

Write a singular noun or a plural noun in the blanks below:

1. I have _____ in my bedroom.
   _{singular noun}

2. There are _____ in the refrigerator.
   _{plural noun}

3. Can you please give me _____?
   _{singular noun}

4. Do you have any _____ in your bag?
   _{plural noun}

5. _____ are very expensive.
   _{plural noun}

6. I found _____ yesterday and I gave it to my
   _{singular noun}
   brother because he doesn't have any _____.
   _{plural noun}

Nouns (4)

I am (I'm)	a student a teacher a drummer	a doctor a farmer a nurse
He is (He's) She is (She's) It is (It's)	a boy a girl a dog	my brother my sister my pet
You are (You're)	a man a woman a singer	my friend my mother my father

****

They are (They're) You are (You're) We are (We're)	students teachers doctors boys girls	dogs brothers sisters friends cats

Fix the mistakes in the sentences below:

1. He a teacher. _____

2. They're student. _____

3. She is my brother. _____

4. We are friend. _____

5. They are a boy. _____

6. She's is a girl. _____

7. Were sisters. _____

Nouns (5)

Nouns are **people**, **places**, or **things.** <u>You can see and touch most nouns.</u>

people	places	things
the student	the bathroom	a dog
my sister	the drugstore	a tennis ball
the baseball player	the USA	a sport
Jane	your house	a bookbag

Circle the nouns in the sentences below:

1. I want to buy medicine at the drugstore.

2. My father is a good tennis player.

3. That girl has a cute dress and a cute bookbag.

4. I want to buy a toy at the department store.

5. My mother gave me some candy.

6. The baseball player lives in the USA.

7. The students are in the classroom.

8. Can I play with your dog?

Nouns (6)

Nouns are **people**, **places**, and **things**. You can see and touch nouns. If there are 2 or more nouns, you add –s to the noun.

There is a	boy girl book table teacher fan pen	car shirt shoe TV bicycle animal pencil	on the _____. under the _____. in the _____. next to the _____. beside the _____. by the _____.
There are	boys girls books tables teachers fans pens	cars shirts shoes TVs bicycles animals pencils	

Fix the mistakes in the sentences below:

1. There is boy in the classroom. _____

2. There is a pencils on the table. _____

3. There are many animal in the zoo. _____

4. There is a fan next to door. _____

5. There books under the table. _____

6. There is a bicycles beside the house. _____

7. There are teacher in the school. _____

Now, look around the classroom, and make 5 sentences of your own!

Nouns (7)

Nouns are **people**, **places**, and **things**. You can see and touch nouns. If there are 2 or more nouns, you add –s to the noun.

There is a	boy girl book table teacher fan pen	car shirt shoe TV bicycle animal pencil	on the _____. under the _____. in the _____. next to the _____. beside the _____. by the _____.
There are	boys girls books tables teachers fans pens	cars shirts shoes TVs bicycles animals pencils	

Now write 5 sentences, using "There is..." or "There are..."

1. _____

2. _____

3. _____

4. _____

5. _____

Nouns (8)

Fix the mistakes in the sentences below.

1. There is three dog in my house.

   _____

2. She is my brother, and he is my sister.

   _____

3. There are a ball in the tree.

   _____

4. They are a boy.

   _____

5. There is a pencils on the table.

   _____

6. He is not my brothers.

   _____

7. There is two cars at my house.

   _____

The Grammar Plan

Part 2

Count / Noncount Nouns

Count / Noncount Nouns (1)

In English, you can count some nouns:

Car	3 cars
House	8 houses
Boy	6 boys
Computer	20 computers

Shirt	2 shirts
Cup	5 cups
Hand	2 hands
Pen	10 pens

(When you have more than one of these "count nouns", you usually add –s or –es.)

But you cannot count some nouns:

Water	Cake	Love
Hair	Juice	Milk
Money	Rice	Food
Corn	Sand	Soup

Look at the nouns below. Circle the Count Nouns.

Cats   Hair   Milk

Keys   TVs

Money   Girls   Cheese

Meat   Monkeys   Hats

Books   Snow   Houses

Pencils   English   Corn

Paper   Desks   Eyes

11

Count / Noncount Nouns (2)

With Count Nouns, you can use the word "many":

Car	**many** cars
House	**many** houses
Boy	**many** boys
Computer	**many** computers

Shirt	**many** shirts
Cup	**many** cups
Hand	**many** hands
Pen	**many** pens

With Noncount Nouns, you can use the word "much":

Water	**much** water
Sand	**much** sand
Money	**much** money
Time	**much** time

Homework	**much** homework
Soup	**much** soup
Snow	**much** snow
Hair	**much** hair

Write "many" or "much" in the blanks below:

1. I don't have _____ hair, but I have _____ cars.

2. She has too _____ corn and too _____ cups.

3. I have too _____ homework! And I don't have _____ time to do it!

4. We don't have _____ money, but we have _____ friends!

Count / Noncount Nouns (3)

You can use "a lot of" with both Count and Noncount Nouns!

Count Nouns

Dog	a lot of dogs
Book	a lot of books
Window	a lot of windows

Friend	a lot of friends
Knife	a lot of knives
Day	a lot of days

Noncount Nouns

Milk	a lot of milk
Cake	a lot of cake
Juice	a lot of juice

Rice	a lot of rice
Love	a lot of love
Money	a lot of money

Fix the mistakes in the sentences below:

1. My friend has a lot of dog.

   _____

2. Julie has a lot of moneys in her pocket.

   _____

3. I am full because I ate a lot of rices for dinner.

   _____

4. There are a lot of window in this room!

   _____

Count / Noncount Nouns (4)

You can use "a lot of" with both Count and Noncount Nouns!

Count Nouns

Dog	many dogs
Book	a lot of books
Window	many windows

Friend	a lot of friends
Knife	many knives
Day	a lot of days

Noncount Nouns

Milk	a lot of milk
Cake	much cake
Juice	a lot of juice

Rice	much rice
Love	a lot of love
Money	much money

Fix the mistakes in the sentences below:

1. Jane has much dogs and many cat in her house.

   _____

2. Mark has too many moneys, but not much times.

   _____

3. Bill drank too many milks and ate too much cake.

   _____

4. I try to read much books every year.

   _____

Count / Noncount Nouns (5)

With Count Nouns, you can use the words "a few":

Car	a few cars
House	a few houses
Bird	a few birds

Shoe	a few shoes
Cup	a few cups
Hand	a few hands

With Noncount Nouns, you can use the words "a little":

Water	a little water
Sand	a little sand
Money	a little money

Time	a little time
Soup	a little soup
Snow	a little snow

Write "a few" or "a little" in the blanks below:

1. Only _____ birds live in the park.

2. You have _____ water on your shirt.

3. I only have _____ time, so I need to do

    _____ work.

4. If you give me _____ cars, I will give you

    _____ money.

5. There are _____ cups on the table.

Count / Noncount Nouns (6)

You can use "some" with both Count and Noncount Nouns!

Count Nouns

Dog	some dogs
Book	some books
Window	some windows

Friend	some friends
Knife	some knives
Day	some days

Noncount Nouns

Milk	some milk
Cake	some cake
Juice	some juice

Rice	some rice
Love	some love
Money	some money

Fix the mistakes in the sentences below:

1. We have some dog and many cat in our house.

   _____

2. I spilled a few juice on some moneys.

   _____

3. We have many time! We can read a little books!

   _____

4. There is some soups and a few waters on the table.

   _____

Count / Noncount Nouns (7)

With Count Nouns, you can use the words "There are":

There are	a few cars
There are	many houses
There are	some birds

There are	a lot of shoes
There are	a few cups
There are	some people

With Noncount Nouns, you can use the words "There is":

There is	a little time
There is	a lot of corn
There is	some milk

There is	some cake
There is	much love
There is	a lot of money

Write 2 sentences with "There is" and 2 sentences with "There are":

Examples:

There is some milk in the kitchen.
There are some shoes in the classroom.

There is:

1. _____

2. _____

There are:

1. _____

2. _____

Count / Noncount Nouns (8)

Fix the mistakes in the following sentences.
If the sentence does not have any mistakes, write *OK*.

1. I have so many homeworks today!

2. There are some cake in the refrigerator.

3. Hurry! We don't have many time! We only have a few minute!

4. There are a lot of cars in the parking lot.

5. There are some pen and a lot of paper in my desk.

6. There is many birds in the park.

7. You need a lot of money if you want to buy many cars.

Count / Noncount Nouns (9)

Some words can be both *Count Nouns* AND *Noncount Nouns*:

There is some chicken. (the food) --------→

There are some chickens. (the animals) ----------------→

There is some pizza. (part of a pizza) -------→

There are some pizzas. (more than one whole pizza) -----→

Draw pictures to show how much/how many there are of the underlined nouns below.

1. There is some **cake** in the refrigerator.

2. There are some **cakes** in the refrigerator.

3. I have a few **chickens** in my house.

Count / Noncount Nouns (10)

You can count Noncount Nouns if you add a measure word:

three | bottles of / glasses of / cups of / drops of | water

four | bowls of / cans of / servings of | soup

two | pieces of / slices of / bites of | pizza

five | pieces of / cans of / plates of / kinds of | corn

Write measure words in the blanks below to complete the sentences.

1. There are six _____ of water in the kitchen.

2. I have seven _____ of chicken on my plate.

3. Can I have one more _____ of rice, please?

4. I drank four _____ of juice last night.

5. Would you like another _____ of soup?

6. I need to buy two _____ of milk.

7. Can I have three _____ of pizza, please?

The Grammar Plan

Part 3

Verbs

Verbs (1)

Verbs are **action words.** <u>Verbs are things that you can do!</u>

- Can you **run**?   Yes!   "**Run**" is a verb!
- Can you **eat**?   Yes!   "**Eat**" is a verb!
- Can you **write**?   Yes!   "**Write** is a verb!

I **You** **We** **They**	**run** **eat** **write** **walk** **go** **play**	(in the park.) (pizza.) (my homework.) (to my house.) (to school.) (with my friend.)

→ With **He**, **She**, and **It**, you have to add –s (or –es) to the verb:

He **She** **It**	**runs** **eats** **writes** **walks** **goes** **plays**	(in the park.) (pizza.) (my homework.) (to my house.) (to school.) (with my friend.)

Circle the verbs in the sentences below:

1. I go to school every day.

2. He eats pizza in the restaurant.

3. They play baseball on Friday.

4. He hit me!

5. You read books very fast!

6. My dog eats a lot of food.

7. The birds fly in the sky.

Verbs (2)

Am, **Is**, and **Are** are verbs, too.
Am, **Is**, and **Are** are called "Be Verbs," because they mean "to be."

- Wrong: I be a girl. (x)
- Right: I **am** a girl.

- Wrong: He be a boy. (x)
- Right: He **is** a boy.

- Wrong: They be students. (x)
- Right: They **are** students.

I	am	a student
He		my brother.
She	is	sleeping.
It		eating food.
You		funny.
We	are	playing a game.
They		brothers.

Write a "be verb" in the blank to complete each sentence:

1. Jimmy and Diana _____ good friends.

2. The teacher _____ looking at the paintings.

3. John and I _____ tired, so we want to sleep.

4. My dog _____ so lazy!

5. I _____ a tall boy.

6. You _____ a cute girl.

7. The bird _____ flying in the sky.

Verbs (3)

Verbs are **action words.** <u>Verbs are things that you can do!</u>

- Can you **think**? Yes! "**Think**" is a verb!
- Can you **drink**? Yes! "**Drink**" is a verb!
- Can you **listen**? Yes! "**Listen** is a verb!

I You We They	**think** **drink** **listen to** **talk** **see**	you are funny! water. music. to my friend. a beautiful bird!

→ With **He**, **She**, and **It**, you have to add –s (or –es) to the verb:

He She It	**thinks** **drinks** **listens to** **talks** **sees**	you are funny! water. music. to my friend. a beautiful bird!

Fix the mistakes in the sentences below:

1. He think English is fun. _____

2. I am go to the park. _____

3. They listens to music every day. _____

4. She is eats breakfast in the morning. _____

5. I thinks you are funny. _____

6. They are talk to my friend. _____

7. My cat eat a lot of food. _____

Verbs (4)

Verbs are **action words.** <u>Verbs are things that you can do!</u>

- Can you **bite**?   Yes!   "**Bite**" is a verb!
- Can you **finish**? Yes!   "**Finish**" is a verb!
- Can you **hope**?   Yes!   "**Hope** is a verb!

I You We They	**finish** **hope** **bite** **save** **need**	(my homework.) (I can go to the zoo.) (the food.) (money in the bank.) (more money.)

→ With **He**, **She**, and **It**, you have to add –s (or –es) to the verb:

He She It	**finishes** **hopes** **bites** **saves** **needs**	(my homework.) (I can go to the zoo.) (the food.) (money in the bank.) (more money.)

Circle the verbs in the sentences below:

1. We finish our homework in the afternoon.

2. He eats pizza in the restaurant.

3. The dog bites the boy's hand.

4. My mother saves money in the bank.

5. You need to finish your homework.

6. Can I play with Jack after school?

7. I hope my mother gives me a toy!

Verbs (5)

Fix the mistakes in the sentences below:

1. My father save his money in the bank.

2. Jenny and Amy is in the restaurant.

3. The brown dog bite the small cat.

4. My brother gos to school every morning at 7:00.

5. David and I am playing in the park.

6. After Joseph finishs his homework, he can play video games.

Verbs (6)

Choose **six** of these verbs, and write a sentence with each one:

share	give	need
save	count	bite
tell	see	hope
finish	ask	borrow
bring	lend	sell
ride	practice	

1. _____

2. _____

3. _____

4. _____

5. _____

6. _____

Nouns and Verbs (Review)

Verbs are **action words**.
Nouns are **people**, **places**, and **things**.

Read the sentences below.
Circle the nouns.
Underline the verbs.

1. The boy buys flowers to give to his mother.

2. The student has a girlfriend.

3. I forgot to bring my pencil box.

4. I will sell you a pencil for 10 dollars.

5. The girls practice English with the foreigner.

6. The man lives in Chicago, but the woman lives in England.

7. There is a storm, so I don't want to play outside.

Nouns and Verbs (Review)

Verbs are **action words**.
Nouns are **people**, **places**, and **things**.

Read the sentences below.
Circle the nouns.
Underline the verbs.

1. He buys flowers for his girlfriend.

2. The dog runs with the cat.

3. I practice baseball after school.

4. I have a birthday present for my mother.

5. Can I borrow a pencil?

6. I hope I can go to Hong Kong.

7. David likes to save money, but his sister likes to spend money.

The Grammar Plan

Part 4

Subjects and Verbs

Subjects and Verbs (1)

The **subject** of a sentence is the most important noun in the sentence.
The **subject** is what the sentence is about.
The **subject** is usually the first noun in the sentence.

My car is dirty.
- What is the sentence about? ("My car")
- The **subject** of the sentence is "car" (or "my car").

I want to go to the USA.
- What is the sentence about? ("I")
- The **subject** of the sentence is "I."

subject	verb	
The dog	**bites**	the boy.
I	**need**	more money.
The bathroom	**is**	too dirty.
Bill	**borrows**	pens every day.
Tennis	**is**	my favorite sport.

Read the sentences below.
Circle the subject.
Underline the verbs.

1. History books are boring.

2. Everyone is different.

3. John and Julie ride their bicycles on the weekend.

4. The teacher lends pencils to the students.

5. The foreigner practices English every afternoon.

Subjects and Verbs (2)

The **subject** of a sentence is the most important noun in the sentence.
The **subject** is what the sentence is about.
The **subject** is usually the first noun in the sentence.

Mexico is a big country.
- What is the sentence about? ("Mexico")
- The **subject** of the sentence is "Mexico."

We will visit my family and drive to the mountains.
- What is the sentence about? ("We")
- The **subject** of the sentence is "We."

subject	verb	
The bookstore	**is**	very far from here.
Taiwan	**is**	a small country.
My family	**likes**	to play outside.
The pizza	**looks**	delicious!
Comic books	**are**	fun to read.

Read the sentences below.
Write a subject in the blank.
Underline the verb.

1. _____ is very tall.

2. _____ can drive a car.

3. _____ is a big country.

4. _____ can fly in the sky.

5. _____ are fun to read.

6. _____ practices English every day.

Subjects and Verbs (3)

Read each sentence.
Circle the subject.
Underline the verb.

1. I am going to the swimming pool.

2. My mother told me that I could play this afternoon.

3. My swimsuit and towel are in my bedroom.

4. My cat is sick, so it doesn't want to eat food.

5. She likes to listen to music.

6. David finishes his homework every day.

7. Linda can swim, but she said the water is too cold.

8. My little brother thinks comic books are interesting.

9. I hope I can go to Mexico someday.

10. Can you lend me your pencil, please?

Subjects and Verbs (4)

Write a subject and a verb in the blanks, to complete each sentence.

1. _____ _____ with my brother.

2. _____ _____ every afternoon.

3. _____ _____ to the beach.

4. _____ _____ after school.

5. _____ _____ with my family on the weekend.

6. _____ _____ every morning.

7. _____ _____ a big country.

8. _____ _____ very dirty.

9. _____ _____ tired, so please be quiet.

10. _____ _____ in the park.

Subjects and Verbs (5)

Choose **six** of the words below. Write a sentence with each word, using it as the **subject** of the sentence.

Example: **bookstore**
   The bookstore is very big.

bookstore	**comic book**	**Everyone**
the USA	**Mexico**	**Taiwan**
towel	**swimming pool**	**swimsuit**
beach	**sand**	**sand castles**
kite	**convenience store**	**batteries**
remote control	**instant noodles**	

1. _____

2. _____

3. _____

4. _____

5. _____

6. _____

Subjects and Verbs (6)

Usually a noun is the subject of a sentence.
If you have a **verb+ing**, it can be the subject of a sentence too!

*If a word ends in **e**, don't write the **e** when you add **–ing**.
- Wrong: Writeing (x)
- Right: Writing

- Wrong: Practiceing (x)
- Right: Practicing

---

subject:

Listening to music	is my hobby.
Playing with fireworks	is dangerous.
Eating fruit	is healthy.
Practicing English	helps me get good grades.
Writing homework	is boring.
Watching TV	is not very fun.
Reading comic books	is one of my hobbies.

Write a subject (**verb+ing**) to complete the sentences below.

1. _____ is my hobby.

2. _____ is interesting.

3. _____ helps me get good grades.

4. _____ is one of my hobbies.

5. _____ is probably dangerous.

6. _____ is not very fun.

7. _____ is healthy.

8. _____ is easy.

Subjects and Verbs (7)

Read each sentence.
Circle the subject.
Underline the verb.

1. Jack reads a book every day.

2. My grandparents agree with my parents.

3. Linda and Lori practice piano every afternoon.

4. Listening to music helps me go to sleep.

5. Playing tennis is Joe's hobby.

6. Wendy draws pictures in her sketch book.

7. Pat walks to the convenience store to buy instant noodles.

8. Jamie thinks history books are interesting.

9. Can I borrow your English book, please?

10. Joe said a funny joke in school today.

The Grammar Plan

Part 5

Adjectives

Adjectives (1)

Adjectives are words that describe nouns. Adjectives make nouns more interesting.

A bird   ->   A big red beautiful bird
My car   ->   My old, dirty car
This story ->   This story is short and funny.

I am (I'm)	big	easy
	small	hard
	short	old
He is (He's)	tall	young
She is (She's)	fun	nice
It is (It's)	boring	mean
	clean	fast
They are (They're)	dirty	slow
You are (You're)		
We are (We're)		

Circle the adjectives in these sentences, and draw an arrow to the noun that they describe.

1. This car is new.

2. She is a funny girl.

3. John is tall, but Jane is short.

4. The new car is very clean.

5. The fast rabbit played with the slow turtle.

6. Playing baseball is very fun!

7. Your book is too dirty! It is not clean!

Adjectives (2)

Opposites are words that have very different meanings. Most adjectives have **opposites**. Match the words with their **opposites** below:

good	**big**
safe	**sad**
happy	**different**
real	**dangerous**
easy	**hard**
fun	**nice**
fast	**bad**
tall	**slow**
young	**short**
mean	**fake**
same	**old**
little	**boring**

Adjectives (3)

In the middle circle, write a **noun.**
In the three outside circles, write three adjectives to describe the noun.

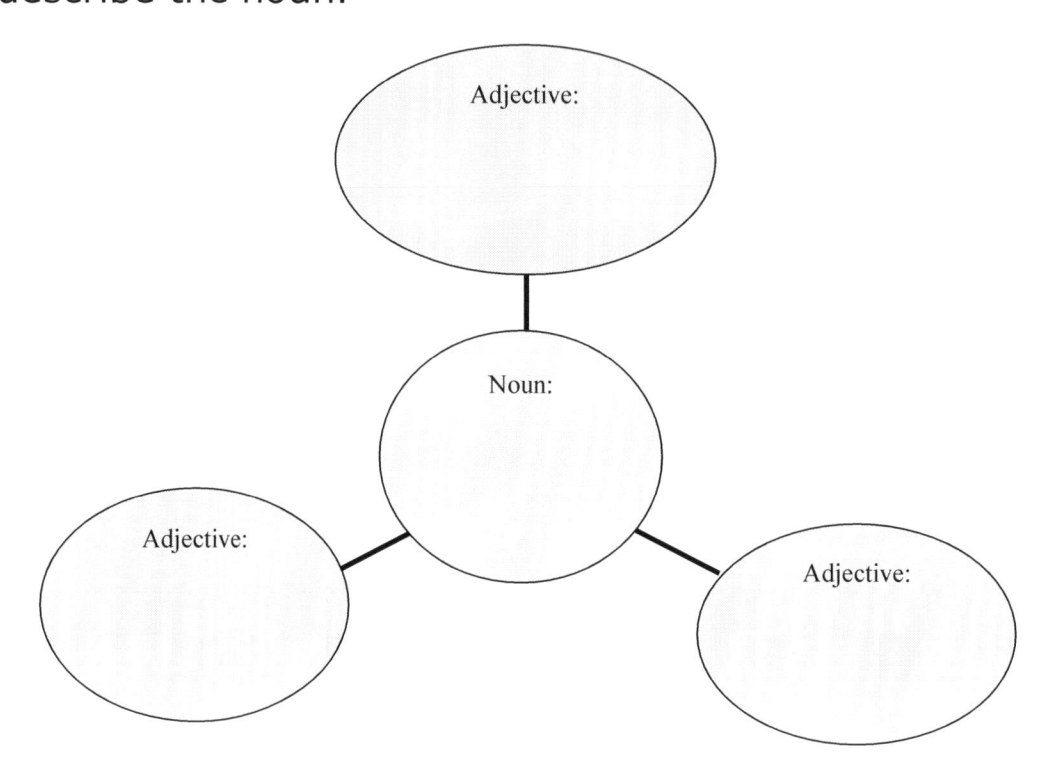

Adjective:

Noun:

Adjective:

Adjective:

Now write 3 sentences, using the words above.

1. _____

2. _____

3. _____

Adjectives (4)

Write an adjective in the blanks below to complete each sentence. (Use a different adjective for each sentence.)

1. My father is _____.

2. The _____ boy can run fast.

3. His pet cat is very _____.

4. I think English is _____.

5. Swimming in the swimming pool is _____.

6. Playing with fireworks is _____.

7. The new car is too _____.

8. I am _____.

9 My grandmother is _____.

10. His girlfriend is very _____.

Adjectives (5)

Circle the adjectives in each sentence, and draw an arrow to the nouns that they describe.

1. Using a computer is difficult.

2. Paper airplanes are fun.

3. I want to buy that new red car.

4. We can use the old paper in my English notebook.

5. The video game is expensive because it is new.

6. Airplanes are fast, but boats are slow.

7. Don't draw disgusting pictures!

8. That picture looks like a real tiger!

9. I think math is easy.

10. The expensive, new car is very fast.

Adjectives (6)

You can also add **–er** to adjectives. "**-er**" means "more." (If you use "adjective + -er, you have to use "than," too.)

- "Bigger" = "more big"
- "Happier" = "more happy"

*If you add –er to an adjective that ends in y, you have to change the y to i, and then write –er.

- Wrong: funnyer (x)
- Right: funnier

My father is	older than	me.
The lion is	bigger than	the rabbit.
Airplanes are	faster than	boats.
My computer is	older than	his computer.
English is	easier than	math.
Winter is	colder than	summer.

Fix the mistakes in the sentences below:

1. I am bigger you. _____

2. The airplane is big than the car._____

3. My dog is funnyer than my cat._____

4. You slower than me. _____

5. English is easy than math. _____

6. My father is younger than my brother. _____

_____

Adjectives (7)

You can also add **–er** to adjectives. "**-er**" means "more." (If you use "adjective + -er, you have to use "than," too.)

- "Bigger" = "more big"
- "Happier" = "more happy"

*If you add –er to an adjective that ends in y, you have to change the y to i, and then write –er.

- Wrong: funnyer (x)
- Right: funnier

The girl is **Comic books are** **Trashcan Dan is** **My sister is**	cuter than funnier than dirtier than nicer than	the boy. history books. Tennis Joe. the bully.

Write **adjective+er (than)** in the blanks to complete each sentence.

1. Airplanes are _____ boats.

2. My father is _____ my sister.

3. I am _____ my teacher.

4. Dolphins are _____ dogs.

5. Math is _____ English.

6. Girls are _____ boys.

7. Summer is _____ winter.

Adjectives (8)

You can also add **–est** to adjectives. "**-est**" means "most."

- "Biggest" = "most big"
- "Happiest" = "most happy"

Complete these sentences:

_____ is the tallest person in the class.

_____ is the oldest person in the class.

_____ is the biggest country.

Complete these sentences using one of these words:

| tallest | oldest | funniest | easiest | biggest |
| shortest | youngest | nicest | hardest | smallest |

I am the _____ person in my family.

My father is the _____ person in my family.

English is the _____ subject in school.

Math is the _____ subject in school.

The teacher is the _____ person in the class.

Brazil is the _____ country in South America.

Russia is the _____ country in the world.

The Grammar Plan

Part 6

Comparative and Superlative Adjectives

Comparative Adjectives (1)

Adjectives are words that describe nouns. Adjectives can also be **Comparative** – this means that they mean "more + adjective."

With most short adjectives (1 or 2 syllables), you add "**-er**."
- big → **bigger**
- funny → **funnier**
- fast → **faster**

With longer adjectives, you add the word "**more**."
- important → **more important**
- interesting → **more interesting**
- beautiful → **more beautiful**

*If an adjective ends in "consonant-y," you have to change the y to i, then add -er. (funnier, easier)

*If an adjective ends in "vowel-consonant," you have to double the consonant, then add –er. (bigger, thinner)

Write the **Comparative** form of the adjectives below:

happy _____   hot _____

comfortable _____   exciting _____

fat _____   sunny _____

silly _____   complicated _____

tall _____   cold _____

intelligent _____   big _____

sad _____   contagious _____

funny _____   ugly _____

crazy _____   pretty _____

cheap _____   disgusting _____

Comparative Adjectives (2)

Fix the mistakes in the sentences below.

1. Riding a rollercoaster is more exciting watching movies.

2. Your English homework is more easy than mine.

3. The white cat is uglyer than the brown cat.

4. The teacher always seems angry, but today she seems angryer than usual.

5. I don't have an air conditioner, so my room is hoter then yours.

6. My new shoes are comfortabler than my old shoes.

7. Fast food is cheaper than home-cooked food, but home-cooked food is more healthy than fast food.

8. You have to be more responsibler with your money!

9. I think that math is more harder then social studies.

Superlative Adjectives (1)

Adjectives can also be **Superlative** – this means that they mean "most + adjective."

With most short adjectives (1 or 2 syllables), you add "**-est**."
- short → the **shortest**
- crazy → the **craziest**
- old → the **oldest**

With longer adjectives, you add the word "**most**."
- exciting → the **most exciting**
- intelligent → the **most intelligent**
- colorful → the **most colorful**

*If an adjective ends in "consonant-y," you have to change the y to i, then add -est. (funniest, easiest)

*If an adjective ends in "vowel-consonant," you have to double the consonant, then add –est. (biggest, thinnest)

Write the **Superlative** form of the adjectives below:

happy _____   hot _____

comfortable _____   exciting _____

fat _____   sunny _____

silly _____   complicated _____

tall _____   cold _____

intelligent _____   big _____

sad _____   considerate _____

funny _____   ugly _____

crazy _____   pretty _____

cheap _____   disgusting _____

Superlative Adjectives (2)

With superlative adjectives, you have to use **the + most/-est**.
With superlative adjectives, you **don't** use the word "than."

- **Wrong:** My dog is biggest dog. (x)
- **Right:**   My dog is <u>the</u> <u>biggest</u> dog.

- **Wrong:** My dog is the biggest than your dog. (x)
- **Right:**   My dog is <u>the</u> <u>biggest</u> dog.
- **Right:**   My dog is bigg<u>er</u> <u>than</u> your dog.

Fix the mistakes in the sentences below.

1. Yesterday was hottest day of the year.
   _____

2. Yesterday was hottest than today.
   _____

3. Elle is most considerate girl in the class.
   _____

4. My mother is the more responsible person in our family.
   _____

5. I think that the brown dog is ugliest than the black dog.
   _____

6. That is dumbest joke I've ever heard!
   _____

7. I didn't get a perfect score because I didn't know the answer to the more complicated question on the test.
   _____

Irregular Adjectives

Some **Comparative** Adjectives are Irregular – this means that the Comparative and Superlative forms are different, and you have to memorize them.

Here is a list of the most common Irregular Adjectives

Adjective	Comparative Form	Superlative Form
good	better	best
bad	worse	worst
far	farther	farthest
fun	more fun	most fun
boring	more boring	most boring
famous	more famous	most famous
ill	worse	worst

Fix the mistakes in the sentences below:

1. Playing baseball is funner than playing basketball.

_____

4. Diana's math score was gooder than mine, but her English score was bader than mine.

_____

_____

3. My computer is gooder than yours, but Julie's new computer is the goodest.

_____

4. Wow! This is the most best movie that I have ever seen!

_____

Adjectives – As---As (1)

To say that 2 things are the same, you use "as [adjective] as."

- My car is big.
  Your car is big, too.
  My car is as big as yours.

- Jake is 14 years old.
  Keith is 14 years old, too.
  Keith is as old as Jake.

Read the sentences below, then write a sentence using "as [adjective] as."

1. Dana's dog is cute.
   Jamie's dog is cute, too.

   _____

2. Chris is responsible.
   His brother is responsible, too.

   _____

3. Sandra's test score is good.
   Tina's test score is good, too.

   _____

4. Joe is 26 years old.
   Paulina is 26 years old, too.

   _____

5. Ryan can run fast.
   Linda can run fast, too.

   _____

6. I think history books are interesting.
   I think comic books are interesting, too.

   _____

Adjectives – As---As (2)

Read the sentences below, then write a sentence using "as [adjective] as" or "more adjective/adjective-er."

1. Dave is 27 years old.
   Julie is 23 years old.

   _____

2. My English test score is 94%.
   Steven's test score is 95%.

   _____

3. Vivian's English test score is 99%.
   Lily's English test score is 99%, too.

   _____

4. Jane's computer is bad.
   Amy's computer is bad, too.

   _____

5. Amy's computer is bad.
   Sally's computer is good.

   _____

6. Fire is hot.
   Ice is cold.

   _____

7. Playing baseball is fun!
   Playing basketball is fun, too!

   _____

Adjectives – As---As (3)

Using the words below, write sentences using "as [adjective] as" or "more adjective/adjective-er."

Example:

bear/tiger

<u>*Tigers are **smaller than** bears.*</u>   *(smaller)*

<u>*Tigers are **as dangerous as** bears.*</u>   *(dangerous)*

1. cell phones / computers

   _____(expensive)

   _____(convenient)

2. You / your teacher

   _____(old)

   _____(short)

3. apples / bananas

   _____(good)

   _____(healthy)

4. motorcycles / cars

   _____(fast)

   _____(dangerous)

Adjectives – Not As---As

You can also say that something is "not as [adjective] as" something else. This is the opposite of "more [adjective]."

- The elephant is **bigger than** the mouse.
    - The mouse is **not as big as** the elephant.

- Your test score is **better than** mine.
    - My test score is **not as good as** yours.

Use "not as [adjective] as" to rewrite the following sentences:

1. John is taller than Stu.

   _____

2. China is bigger than Taiwan.

   _____

3. Randy's cell phone is newer than mine.

   _____

4. I think that history is more interesting than science.

   _____

5. Black and white movies are worse than color movies.

   _____

6. Apples are healthier than candy.

   _____

7. Dogs are noisier than cats.

   _____

Adjectives – Review

Complete the sentences below, using one of the following patterns:

- **more adjective than / adjective+er than**
- **as adjective as**
- **not as adjective as**

1. (interesting)

I think that math is _____ science.

I think that science is _____ math.

2. (fast / slow)

Rabbits are _____ turtles.

Turtles are _____ rabbits.

3. (old / young)

My mother is _____ my father.

My teacher is _____ I am.

I am _____ my teacher.

4. (healthy)

Bananas are _____ oranges.

Candy is _____ bananas.

5. (fun / boring)

Playing outside is _____ doing homework.

Playing baseball is _____ playing tennis.

6. (hot / cold)

Summer is _____ winter.

Winter is _____ summer.

7. (quiet / noisy)

Dogs are _____ cats.

Cats are _____ dogs.

Cars are _____ bicycles.

Bicycles are _____ cars.

8. (young / old)

I am _____ my parents.

My parents are _____ my grandparents.

Babies are _____ adults.

My teacher is _____ I am.

9. (stinky)

Flowers are _____ my dirty socks.

My dirty socks are _____ flowers.

10. (cheap / expensive)

Pencils are _____ books.

Cell phones are _____ computers.

11. (responsible)

My friend is _____ me.

I am _____ my friend.

12. (expensive / cheap)

The imported washing machine is _____ the washing machine that is made in this country.

The second-hand washing machine is _____ the new washing machine.

The Grammar Plan

Part 7

Adverbs

Adverbs (1)

You know that adjectives are words that modify nouns.
Adverbs are words that can modify verbs, adjectives, or other adverbs. In this section, we will focus on adverbs that modify verbs.

- I run **slowly**. ("slowly" modifies "run.")
- He writes **neatly**. ("neatly" modifies "writes.")
- Please drive **carefully**. ("carefully" modifies "drive.")

*****Most (but not all) adverbs end in "-ly."**

Look at the sentences below. Can you find the adverbs? Circle the adverbs, and draw an arrow to the verbs that they modify.

1. Derek rides his bicycle very quickly.

2. Monica talks too quietly, so I can't hear what she is saying.

3. I accidentally hit James, so I said I was sorry.

4. My mother drives very carefully because she doesn't want to have another accident.

5. Wow! Henry sings beautifully!

6. The two girls are playing happily in the park.

7. Doris' father angrily yelled at her last night.

8. We were walking slowly when it started to rain.

9. The teacher was angry because I wrote my homework carelessly.

Adverbs (2)

Game 1
Choose one verb from the list on the left, and one adverb from the list on the right. Then choose one student in your class (or your teacher!), and they have to act out the words that you say.

Examples: Run quickly
　　　　　Speak beautifully

Verbs	Adverbs
walk	quickly
run	slowly
eat	loudly
speak	quietly
dance	carefully
sing	recklessly
write	beautifully
sleep	sadly
sit	happily
stand	angrily

Game 2 – Charades
Divide the class into two teams. The teacher will call one student from one team to the front of the class, and show him one verb and one adverb (for example: run angrily). The student must act these words out. If his/her team can guess the two words, the team gets one point.

After everyone has acted, count the points and see which team won!

Adverbs (3)

Write an adverb in each blank to complete each sentence. (Each sentence should **make sense!**)

1. Rabbits can jump very _____.

2. That baby is crying so _____.

3. Jack drives too _____, so the police officer gave him a ticket.

4. Please don't talk so _____. Some people are still taking a test.

5. The roads are very wet, so please drive _____.

6. You are speaking too _____; I can't hear you!

7. After Jessica had a fight with her friend, she walked home _____.

8. Wow! I didn't know your sister could sing so _____.

9. My English teacher talks too _____, so he is very hard to understand.

10. You should write your homework _____ so you don't make mistakes.

Adverbs (4)

Not all adverbs end in **"-ly."** Here are some **Irregular Adverbs** that don't end in –ly.

far (I can run very far.)
fast (I can run very fast.)
hard (John hit me very hard.)
high (The plane is flying very high.)
late (I finished late.)
long (I slept very long last night.)
low (The plane is flying very low.)
well (She can sing very well.)

   *Don't forget: **good** is an adjective, **well** is an adverb

Fix the mistakes in the following sentences:

1. My English teacher speaks too fastly, so I can't understand him.

_____

2. Kate drives careful because she doesn't want to have an accident.

_____

3. Brian came to school lately today.

_____

4. We ran very farly after school, so I am pretty tired.

_____

5. The teacher yelled angry at the bully.

_____

6. Chris and Danny can play baseball very good.

_____

7. You should speak more quiet when you go to the library.

_____

Adverbs (5)

***Be careful!** Some adverbs can be very confusing:
The word **hardly** means **the opposite of hard**, or "barely."
- **David hit me hard!** (It hurts a lot!)
- **David hardly hit me!** (It doesn't hurt at all.)
(Sometimes people greet each other by saying, **"Are you working hard, or hardly working."** What do you think this means?)

The word **lately** means **"recently."**
- **Vicky was late to school today.** (She was not early.)
- **Vicky has been tired lately.** (She has been tired recently - for a few days or weeks.)

Fill in the blanks with **hard, hardly, late, or lately.**

1. Jenna is working very _____ right now, so please don't bother her.

2. Jason is _____ working right now, so you can bother him if you want.

3. I have been taking many tests _____, so I have been studying very hard.

4. I came to class _____ because my mother drives too slowly.

5. It's _____ raining, so I think I will walk to school.

6. It's raining too _____! Can you drive me to school today?

7. I have been working late _____, so I haven't had enough time to sleep.

8. James _____ studies for his tests, so his grades are getting worse and worse.

Adverbs (6)

Be careful! Some adverbs can be very confusing:
Many people confuse the words "good" and "well." Don't forget:

"Good" is an adjective, and "well" is an adverb.
- I am a good baseball player.
- I can play baseball well.
- My math score was very good.
- I do well on math tests.

Bad is an adjective, and "badly" is an adverb.
- I think that is a bad movie.
- Jane doesn't want to sing because she sings badly.
- My English score was so bad!
- I always do badly on science tests.

Write "good," "well," "bad," or "badly" in the blanks below.

1. I won't eat your food because you don't cook _____.

2. I play tennis very _____, so I always lose.

3. This hamburger is _____! I can't eat it!

4. Leo dances very _____! He is so talented!

5. She can't speak English very _____, so she is shy to talk to foreigners.

6. I tried to draw a dog, but I draw so _____ that it looks like a cat!

7. This salad is really _____! You should try it!

Adjective or Adverb?

Directions:
1.) Underline each adjective and draw and arrow to the noun that it modifies.

2.) Circle each adverb and draw an arrow to the verb it modifies.

1. The test was difficult so I wrote the answers quickly.

2. The red car can go fast.

3. The fast car is red.

4. He translates accurately but he speaks too quickly.

5. I write more slowly than Jane, but Jane's words are messy.

6. The fat cat quietly ran across the dirty floor.

7. She correctly answered the easy questions, but she incorrectly answered the hard ones.

8. The beautiful dancer moves gracefully in a cute dress.

9. She dances terribly and her voice is horrible.

10. Speak softly and carry a big stick.

The Grammar Plan

Part 8

Appendix and Answer Key

List of 100 Common Nouns

1. word
2. letter
3. number
4. person
5. pen
6. class
7. people
8. sound
9. water
10. side
11. place
12. man
13. men
14. woman
15. women
16. boy
17. girl
18. year
19. day
20. week
21. month
22. name
23. sentence
24. line
25. air
26. land
27. home
28. hand
29. house
30. picture
31. animal
32. mother
33. father
34. brother
35. sister
36. world
37. head
38. page
39. country
40. question
41. answer
42. school
43. plant
44. food
45. sun
46. state
47. eye
48. city
49. tree
50. farm
51. story
52. sea
53. night
54. day
55. life
56. north
57. south
58. east
59. west
60. child
61. children
62. example
63. paper
64. music
65. river
66. car
67. foot
68. feet
69. book
70. science
71. room
72. friend
73. idea
74. fish
75. mountain
76. horse
77. watch
78. color
79. face
80. wood
81. list
82. bird
83. body
84. dog
85. family
86. song
87. door
88. product
89. wind
90. ship
91. area
92. rock
93. order
94. fire
95. problem
96. piece
97. top
98. bottom
99. king
100. space

List of 100 Common Verbs

1. agree
2. ask
3. become
4. believe
5. bite
6. borrow
7. break
8. bring
9. brush
10. buy
11. cancel
12. change
13. clean
14. climb
15. close
16. complain
17. count
18. cure
19. cut
20. cry
21. dance
22. draw
23. drink
24. drive
25. eat
26. explain
27. fall
28. find
29. finish
30. fix
31. fly
32. forget
33. give
34. go
35. have
36. hear
37. hide
38. hold
39. hope
40. ignore
41. know
42. learn
43. leave
44. lend
45. listen
46. live
47. look
48. lose
49. make
50. need
51. open
52. pay
53. play
54. practice
55. pretend
56. promise
57. put
58. rain
59. read
60. ride
61. run
62. save
63. say
64. see
65. sell
66. share
67. sing
68. sit
69. sleep
70. speak
71. spell
72. spend
73. stand
74. start
75. steal
76. study
77. swim
78. take
79. talk
80. teach
81. tease
82. tell
83. think
84. throw
85. translate
86. travel
87. trust
88. try
89. turn off
90. turn on
91. understand
92. use
93. wait
94. wake up
95. walk
96. want
97. watch
98. work
99. worry
100. write

List of 100 Common Adjectives

1. afraid
2. alive
3. angry
4. annoyed
5. annoying
6. apart
7. bad
8. beautiful
9. big
10. boring
11. broken
12. busy
13. cheap
14. clear
15. close
16. closed
17. cold
18. cool
19. dangerous
20. dark
21. dead
22. different
23. done
24. dry
25. early
26. easy
27. empty
28. excited
29. exciting
30. expensive
31. fake
32. false
33. far
34. fast
35. few
36. fine
37. finished
38. first
39. flat
40. free
41. full
42. good
43. great
44. happy
45. hard
46. hard
47. heavy
48. high
49. hot
50. huge
51. interesting
52. large
53. last
54. last
55. late
56. light
57. light
58. little
59. long
60. low
61. many
62. mean
63. near
64. new
65. next
66. nice
67. noisy
68. old
69. old
70. open
71. poor
72. pretty
73. quick
74. ready
75. real
76. rich
77. right
78. sad
79. safe
80. same
81. short
82. slow
83. small
84. soft
85. special
86. strange
87. strong
88. sure
89. surprised
90. tall
91. tiny
92. tired
93. together
94. true
95. ugly
96. warm
97. weak
98. wet
99. wrong
100. young

Answer Key

Many of the worksheets in this book have many possible answers. This answer key provides sample answers. Students' answers may vary.

page 2
1. I, department store
2. doctor, teacher, car
3. book, classroom
4. cat, bed
5. house, England
6. I, medicine
7. You, animals, zoo
8. Elle, dress

page 3
1. I want to go to the library.
2. The cat and the dog are in the car.
3. There is a big spider in the classroom.
4. The dog likes to sit on the bed.
5. My sister is in England.
6. I want to buy some bread.
7. You can see animals in a zoo.
8. Hi Elle. Your shirt is very cute.

page 4
1. I have a hat in my bedroom.
2. There are apples in the refrigerator.
3. Can you please give me a pen?
4. Do you have any erasers in your bag?
5. Cars are very expensive.
6. I found a novel yesterday, and I gave it to my brother because he doesn't have any books.

page 5
1. He's a teacher.
2. They're students.
3. She is my sister.
4. We are friends.
5. They are boys.
6. She's a girl.
7. We're sisters.

page 6
1. I, medicine, drugstore
2. father, tennis player
3. girl, dress, bookbag
4. I, toy, department store
5. mother, candy
6. baseball player, USA
7. students, classroom
8. I, dog

page 7
1. There is a boy in the classroom.
2. There is a pencil on the table.
3. There are many animals in the zoo.
4. There is a fan next to the door.
5. There are books under the table.
6. There is a bicycle beside the house.
7. There are teachers in the school.

page 8
1. There is a fan on the wall.
2. There are books on the shelves.
3. There is a bicycle on the sidewalk.
4. There are TVs in the store.
5. There is a table next to the door.

page 9
1. There are three dogs in my house.
2. She is my sister, and he is my brother.
3. There is a ball in the tree.
4. They are boys.
5. There is a pencil on the table.
6. He is not my brother.
7. There are two cars at my house.

page 11
Count Nouns: Cats, Keys, TVs, Girls, Monkeys, Hats, Books, Houses, Pencils, Desks, Eyes

page 12
1. I don't have much hair, but I have many cars.
2. She has too much corn and too many cups.
3. I have too much homework! And I don't have much time to do it!
4. We don't have much money, but we have many friends!

page 13
1. My friend has a lot of dogs.
2. Julie has a lot of money in her pocket.
3. I am full because I ate a lot of rice for dinner.
4. There are a lot of windows in this room!

page 14
1. Jackie has a lot of dogs and cats in her house.
2. Mark has too much money, but not much time.
3. Bill drank too much milk and ate too much cake.
4. I try to read many books every year.

page 15
1. a few
2. a little
3. a little, a little
4. a few, a little
5. a few

page 16
1. We have some dogs and many cats in our house.
2. I spilled a little juice on some money.
3. We have much time! We can read a few books!
4. There is some soup and a little water on the table.

page 17
There is:
1. There is a little orange juice in the refrigerator.
2. There is a lot of corn on the table.
There are:
1. There are many houses on this street.
2. There are a few birds in the tree.

page 18
1. I have so much homework today!
2. There is some cake in the refrigerator.
3. Hurry! We don't have much time! We only have a few minutes!
4. OK
5. There are some pens and a lot of paper in my desk.
6. There are many birds in the park.
7. OK

71

page 19
1.
2.
3.

page 20
1. bottles / cups / glasses
2. pieces
3. bowl / serving
4. glasses / bottles / cups
5. bowl / cup / serving
6. gallons / bottles / glasses
7. pieces / slices

page 22
1. go 2. eats 3. play 4. hit 5. read 6. eats 7. fly

page 23
1. are 2. is 3. are 4. is 5. am 6. are 7. is

page 24
1. He thinks English is fun.
2. I am going to the park.
3. They listen to music every day.
4. She eats breakfast in the morning.
5. I think you are funny.
6. They talk to my friend.
7. My cat eats a lot of food.

page 25
1. finish   2. eats   3. bites   4. saves
5. need, finish   6. play   7. hope, gives

page 26
1. My father saves his money in the bank.
2. Jenny and Amy are in the restaurant.
3. The brown dog bites the small cat.
4. My brother goes to school every morning at 7:00.
5. David and I are playing in the park.
6. After Joseph finishes his homework, he can play video games.

page 27
1. My father tells me many interesting stories.
2. I hope you can come to my house tomorrow.
3. Jason borrows a pencil from me every day.
4. My aunt and uncle sell cars.
5. We finish our homework every evening.
6. Kate rides her bike in the park on the weekends.

page 28
1. Nouns: boy, flowers, mother   Verbs: buys, give
2. Nouns: student, girlfriend   Verbs: has
3. Nouns: I, pencil box   Verbs: forgot, bring
4. Nouns: I, you, pencil, dollars   Verbs: sell
5. Nouns: girls, English, foreigner Verbs: practice
6. Nouns: man, Chicago, woman, England   Verbs: lives, lives
7. Nouns: storm, I, outside   Verbs: is, want, play

page 29
1. Nouns: He, flowers, girlfriend   Verbs: buys
2. Nouns: dog, cat   Verbs: runs
3. Nouns: I, baseball, school   Verbs: practice

4. Nouns: I, birthday present, mother   Verbs: have
5. Nouns: I, pencil   Verbs: borrow
6. Nouns: I, I, Hong Kong   Verbs: hope, go
7. Nouns: David, money, sister, money   Verbs: likes, save, likes, spend

page 31
1. Subject: History books   Verb: are
2. Subject: Everyone   Verb: is
3. Subject: John and Julie   Verb: ride
4. Subject: teacher   Verb: lends
5. Subject: foreigner   Verb: practices

page 32
1. My grandfather 2. My sister 3. Canada 4. Birds
5. Comic books 6. Jane

page 33
1. Subject: I   Verb: am going
2. Subject: My mother   Verb: told
3. Subject: My swimsuit and towel   Verb: are
4. Subject: My cat   Verb: is
5. Subject: She   Verb: likes
6. Subject: David   Verb: finishes
7. Subject: Linda   Verb: swim
8. Subject: My little brother   Verb: thinks
9. Subject: I   Verb: hope
10. Subject: you   Verb: lend

page 34
1. Jack plays
2. We swim
3. My family goes
4. Amanda studies
5. Uncle Mark visits
6. We jog
7. Brazil is
8. This room is
9. I am
10. Those cats live

page 35
1. This bookstore is my favorite place.
2. The USA is a big country.
3. This towel is wet.
4. Mexico is far away.
5. The swimming pool is round.
6. Everyone likes ice cream!

page 36
1. Playing basketball
2. Listening to his stories
3. Reading
4. Riding a bicycle
5. Touching that fish
6. Cleaning my room
7. Eating vegetables
8. Finishing this English worksheet

page 37
1. Subject: Jack   Verb: reads
2. Subject: My grandparents   Verb: agree
3. Subject: Linda and Lori   Verb: practice
4. Subject: Listening to music   Verb: helps
5. Subject: Playing tennis   Verb: is
6. Subject: Wendy   Verb: draws
7. Subject: Pat   Verb: walks
8. Subject: Jamie   Verb: thinks
9. Subject: I   Verb: borrow
10. Subject: Joe   Verb: said

page 39
1. new -> car
2. funny -> girl
3. tall -> John, short -> Jane
4. new -> car, clean -> car
5. fast -> rabbit, slow -> turtle
6. fun -> playing baseball

page 40
Opposites:
good – bad
safe – dangerous
happy – sad
real – fake
easy – hard
fun – boring
fast – slow
tall – short
young – old
mean – nice
same – different
little – big

page 41

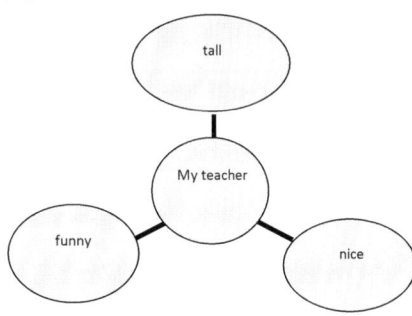

1. My teacher is tall.
2. My teacher is funny.
3. My teacher is nice.

page 42
1. tall 2. short 3. noisy 4. fun 5. tiring
6. dangerous 7. expensive 8. tired 9. kind 10. pretty

page 43
1. difficult -> using a computer
2. fun -> paper airplanes
3. new -> car, red -> car
4. old -> paper
5. expensive -> video game, new -> video game
6. fast -> airplanes, slow -> boats
7. disgusting -> pictures
8. real -> tiger
9. easy -> math
10. expensive -> car, new -> car, fast -> car

page 44
1. I am bigger than you.
2. The airplane is bigger than the car.
3. My dog is funnier than my cat.
4. You are slower than me.
5. English is easier than math.
6. My father is older than my brother.

page 45
1. faster than / bigger than
2. older than / taller than
3. younger than / shorter than / noisier than

4. bigger than / cuter than
5. easier than / harder than
6. nicer than / funnier than / shorter than
7. hotter than / better than

page 48
happier   hotter
more comfortable   more exciting
fatter   sunnier
sillier   more complicated
taller   colder
more intelligent   bigger
sadder   more contagious
funnier   uglier
crazier   prettier
cheaper   more disgusting

page 49
1. Riding a rollercoaster is more exciting than watching movies.
2. Your English homework is easier than mine.
3. The white cat is uglier than the brown cat.
4. The teacher always seems angry, but today she seems angrier than usual.
5. I don't have an air conditioner, so my room is hotter than yours.
6. My new shoes are more comfortable than my old shoes.
7. Fast food is cheaper than home-cooked food, but home-cooked food is healthier than fast food.
8. You have to be more responsible with your money.
9. I think that math is harder than social studies.

page 50
the happiest   the hottest
the most comfortable   the most exciting
the fattest   the sunniest
the silliest   the most complicated
the tallest   the coldest
the most intelligent   the biggest
the saddest   the most considerate
the funniest   the ugliest
the craziest   the prettiest
the cheapest   the most disgusting

page 51
1. Yesterday was the hottest day of the year.
2. Yesterday was hotter than today.
3. Elle is the most considerate girl in the class.
4. My mother is the most responsible person in our family.
5. I think that the brown dog is uglier than the black dog.
6. That is the dumbest joke I've ever heard!
7. I didn't get a perfect score because I didn't know the answer to the most complicated question on the test.

page 52
1. Playing baseball is more fun than playing basketball.
2. Diana's math score was better than mine, but her English score was worse than mine.
3. My computer is better than yours, but Julie's new computer is the best.
4. Wow! This is the best movie that I have ever seen!

page 53
1. Dana's dog is as cute as Jamie's dog.
2. Chris is as responsible as his brother.
3. Sandra's test score is as good as Tina's.
4. Joe is as old as Paulina.
5. Ryan can run as fast as Linda.
6. I think history books are as interesting as comic books.

page 54
1. Dave is older than Julie.

2. My English test score is lower than Steven's.
3. Vivian's English test score is as high as Lily's.
4. Jane's computer is as bad as Amy's.
5. Amy's computer is worse than Sally's.
6. Fire is hotter than ice.
7. Playing baseball is as fun as playing basketball.

page 55
1. Computers are more expensive than cell phones.
   Cell phones are more convenient than computers
2. Your teacher is older than you.
   You are shorter than your teacher.
3. Apples are as good as bananas.
   Apples are as healthy as bananas.
4. Cars are faster than motorcycles.
   Motorcycles are more dangerous than cars.

page 56
1. Stu is not as tall as John.
2. Taiwan is not as big as China.
3. My cell phone is not as new as Randy's.
4. I think that science is not as interesting as history.
5. Color movies are not as bad as black and white movies.
6. Candy is not as healthy as apples.
7. Cats are not as noisy as dogs.

page 57
1. more interesting than, not as interesting as
2. faster than, slower than
3. older than, older than, younger than
4. as healthy as, not as healthy as
5. not as boring as, not as fun as
6. not as cold as, not as hot as

page 58
7. not as quiet as, not as noisy as, noisier than, quieter than
8. younger than, not as old as, younger than, older than
9. not as stinky as, stinkier than
10. cheaper than, not as expensive as
11. more responsible than, not as responsible as
12. more expensive than, cheaper than

page 60
1. quickly -> rides
2. quietly -> talks
3. accidentally -> hit
4. carefully -> drives
5. beautifully -> sings
6. happily -> playing
7. angrily -> yelled
8. slowly ->walking
9. carelessly -> wrote

page 62
1. quickly   2. loudly   3. carelessly   4. loudly   5. carefully
6. quietly   7. quickly   8. beautifully   9. quickly   10. carefully

page 63
1. My English teacher speaks too fast, so I can't understand him.
2. Kate drives carefully because she doesn't want to have an accident.
3. Brian came to school late today.
4. We ran very far after school, so I am pretty tired.
5. The teacher yelled angrily at the bully.
6. Chris and Danny can play baseball very well.
7. You should speak more quietly when you go to the library.

page 64
1. hard   2. hardly   3. lately   4. late
5. hardly   6. hard   7. lately   8. hardly

page 65
1. well   2. badly   3. bad   4. well   5. well   6. badly   7. good

page 66
1. Adjective: difficult -> test   Adverb: quickly -> wrote
2. Adjective: red -> car   Adverb: fast -> go
3. Adjective: fast -> car, red -> car   Adverb: (none)
4. Adjective: (none)   Adverb: accurately -> translates, quickly -> speaks
5. Adjective: messy -> words   Adverb: slowly -> write
6. Adjective: fat -> cat, dirty -> floor   Adverb: quietly -> ran
7. Adjective: easy -> questions, hard -> ones   Adverb: correctly -> answered, incorrectly -> answered
8. Adjective: beautiful -> dancer, cute -> dress   Adverb: gracefully -> moves
9. Adjective: horrible -> voice   Adverb: terribly -> dances
10. Adjective: big -> stick   Adverb: softly -> speak

Made in United States
Orlando, FL
01 June 2023